I Only Work Here

US ARMY

10DD-001

I ONLY WORK HERE

Five Decades of Poetry
in Four Styles

Ernest M. Robson
Marion Robson

DUFOUR EDITIONS, INC.

ACKNOWLEDGEMENT

Nine of the compositions in this book were published as poster poems by the MIDDLE EARTH BOOK SHOP, Philadelphia, 1973. These colored posters were designed by Sam and Syms Amico in a limited edition of one hundred in hand made portfolios.

First published 1975 by

DUFOUR EDITIONS, INC.

Booksellers and Publishers

Chester Springs, Pa. 19425

ISBN 0 8023 1258 6 — cloth

ISBN 0 8023 1259 4 — paper

Copyright© 1975 Ernest and Marion Robson

Library of Congress Catalog Card Number 74-18635

OTHER TITLES BY ERNEST ROBSON

THE ORCHESTRA OF THE LANGUAGE, 1959

TRANSWHICHICS, 1970

THOMAS ONETWO, 1971

Printed in the United States
by Smale's Printery, Inc.
Pottstown, Pa.

CONTENTS

APPENDIX

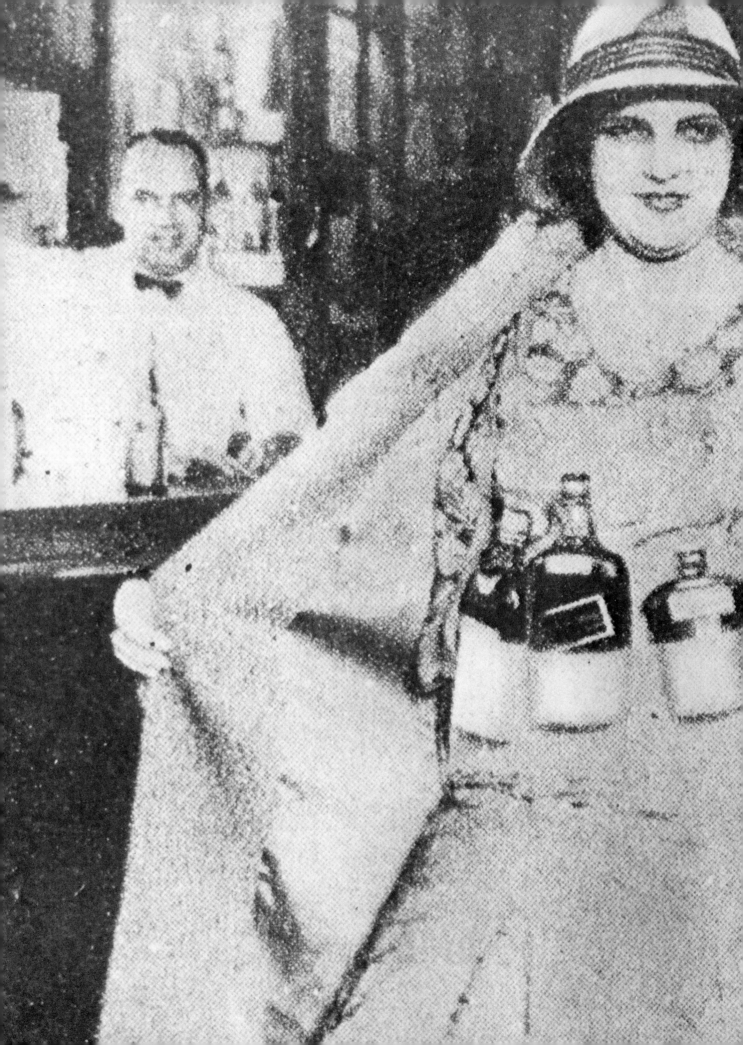

STATEMENT

Nine of the compositions in this book were published as poster poems by the MIDDLE EARTH BOOK SHOP, Philadelphia, 1973. These colored posters were designed by Sam and Sims Amico in a limited edition of 100 and distributed in handmade portfolios.

INTRODUCTION

out of nowhere which must be somewhere
came Ernest Robson with Thomas Onetwo,
Transwichics, and now his most recent
offering, I Only Work Here.

he revealed himself and his work to me one
strange sunny new york afternoon. since
then i have found myself with a new friend
who makes frequent calls and pays
occasional visits.

who is Ernest Robson? he is an
underground merlin, the original wild man,
mad poet, a struggle to be me, a mole,
astronomer, furtrapper, romantic
revolutionary, scientist, marxist cannibal,
a genuine profound character, an
anachronism in his time.

at first glance to the inexperienced eye his
poetry might seem weird, superficial and
trite, but upon a more thorough continued
analysis you get lost finding (before you
know it) a cosmic path to new realities
in new forms of poetry.

his own invention and discovery, the
prosodynic print is an incredible advance
in the information of language. like a
delicate line drawing with variety in texture
and line value, affecting the tone, rhythm,
imagery, and the pitch of the sound.

upon hearing the poems (read them to
yourself) you find a dear, sensitive, kind,
sometimes angry, loving man doing his
thing with style.

unknown except to sophisticated small
circles, unrealized, hilarious and subtle with
praise long overdue, I Only Work Here by
Ernest Robson, although sometimes
esoteric, is an incredible learning
experience.

a life chronical of man and woman kind,
the travels of a visionary poet.

reader you can't be casual with this unique
work. you'll have to think, if you want to dig
what's happening. give yourself a special
time consuming task treat. let the ben
franklin, engles, charles ives, galileo,
daniel boone, mao tse-tung and groucho
marx in Ernest Robson blow your mind.
i did and it was great.

w. bliem kern   1st february e 1974   new york city

AUTHOR'S INTRODUCTION

The reader may judge more fairly the quality of this book when its intentions are known.

There are criteria for poetic excellence which have been applied rigorously in some compositions, loosely in others. They may be epitomized in two statements: poetry in contrast to prose fiction is a *physical language art* that maximizes information with minimum statement. In contrast to theatre, poetry is primarily a language art designed to arouse interest, pleasure, and discovery in pattern recognitions within language and by means of language.

It is also a paraphrase art that repeats the same theme over centuries in a different form. When poetry reorders old experience, it is a redundancy. Unfortunately, most of academia has perpetuated this redundancy at the expense of information by converting poetry into a museum study.

There are three ways poetry may contribute information. One is to increase *the number of ways of writing,* i.e. the number of symbols *a poet might compose to convey a theme.* The symbols may be physical as in this book. A second manner of increasing the information of poetry is to acquire new observations through the magnified perceptibility of scientific instruments (telescopes, microscopes, spectrographs, etc.) A third road to new information is through a multiple diversity of authorial experiences, which the average citizen is not likely to encompass in a single life.

This book results from taking these three approaches to information.

To carry out this principle four styles of script were used. They express images, notes, observations and passages made through five decades, 1923 through 1973. Since the main interest is in poetry itself, rather than history or autobiography, the quality of the specific composition or poem was the first consideration. A second consideration was the clustering of poems in sections around themes or moods or refrains.

Although the historical interest is secondary throughout this book, it is still there. Accordingly, the numbers that appear after each composition identify the year when observations or images or concepts or compositions were recorded: i.e. 25-73 indicates that work was done on the poem in 1925 and 1973. Obviously it was completed in 1973. Three sets of numbers 29-39-71 show the composition was worked on during those three years and completed in the last year.

The modified template techniques for orthography, line shape and page beauty of a poem, created by Marion Robson, liberates the poet from slavery to the typewriter. The typewriter is surely a restriction on the potentials of visual poetry. Why shouldn't other people, along with the orientals, write poetry as a creative visual experience as well as an audio-vocal art?

The final justification for publication is that the writing is both a singular and synergistic creation of two very different minds reflecting five decades of varied and multiple experiences. Neither one of the two authors could have composed this book alone.

ERNEST M. ROBSON

I Only Work Here

Litany for the Disturbed

WEEP FOR THE WOMB — CHILDREN,
EITHER LIKE ACTORS WITHOUT AUDIENCES
THEY STALK ACROSS THE FLOORS OF EMPTY HALLS
POURING FORTH THEIR SPEECH IN VAIN,
OR, WITH CHIN AGAINST THEIR KNEES THEY SIT
LIKE CRICKETS FROZEN IN THE SNOW.

WEEP FOR THE WOMB — CHILDREN,
FOR THOUGH THEY SEE IMMORTAL COWS STANDING
ON A ROAD AS SMOOTH AS MUSIC
IN A MIST OF LAVENDER
AND EVEN THOUGH THEY SEE THEIR LOVE
"RISE OUT OF THE GREEN GRASS AND SING":

DO WEEP FOR THE WOMB — CHILDREN,
FOR THEY ARE TRYING TO STAND ALONE
ON WHITE PLACES UNDER THE SUN,
HOPING TO ATONE
FOR EVIL THINGS
THEY HAVE NOT DONE.

26

Psycho-Analysts

> 600 cases, 1937-45 CAMBRIDGE-SOMERVILLE YOUTH STUDY on prevention of juvenile delinquency in under-privileged boys.		
	Psychiatric Guidance:	With NO Psychiatric Guidance:
	test group	control group
Offenses	264	218
Court Appearances	96	92

150 cases, 1955 BARRON-LEARY STUDY of psycho-analytically oriented therapies of in-clinic patients on basis of the Minnesota Multi-Phase Personality Treatment.

INTERVALS OF STUDY

7:00 months for non-treatment group
8:23 months for individual therapy group
8:63 months for group therapy group

RESULTS

NO SIGNIFICANT DIFFERENCES in magnitude or direction of changes in groups.

> 900 cases, 1955 BRILL-BEEBE STUDY OF THERAPY in treatments of war neuroses in soldiers matched for: areas of stress; preservice personality and impairments; severity of breakdown.

TREATMENTS	RESULTS
A. Nothing more than Rest and Sedation B. Individual Therapy C. Hospital Routine	NO significant differences between A, B, and C.

AFTER **STATISTICS** SHOW
THEIR **THERAPY** NO BETTER THAN **CHANCE**,
WE LOOKED INSIDE THEIR **SKULLS** TO SEE
WHAT **TREASURES** JUSTIFIED THEIR **FEE**.
EXCUSE ME FRIENDS FOR BEING SO **BLUNT**,
I COULDN'T FIND MUCH MORE **INSIDE**
THAN MIDDLE **CLASS** VIENNA **GAS**
ABOUT A **CUNT**.

25-72-73

FOR VERIFICATION OF ABOVE DATA SEE:
"Handbook of Abnormal Psychology", 1961,
Basic Books, N.Y. Chapter 18, pages 697-725,
H. J. Eysenck PhD, Editor.

Lines to Three Doctors

THE **DOORS** THAT **GUARD** THE **PATHWAYS** TO THE **BRAIN**

OPEN TO **POLAR** KEYS ON **CARBON** CHAINS,

OVER THRESHOLDS STUMBLE–THUMPED WITH **PAIN** .

SHOUTS SCREAMS . . . .

SHATTERED WHEN TORRENTS OF **NOISE**

ON HOT BRIGHT STREAMS

RUSH IN . . . . IN TRILLIONS . . . . AS THO **STRUCK** BY THE **SUN**

OR . . . . WHEN THOSE **CHEMIC KEYS** TUNE IN

WITH RESONANT **AMINES**

WHAT **AWESOME** ORCHESTRATIONS MAY ARISE

TO **LIFT** THE **GATES** BEHIND THE **EYES** . . . . .

AND **STRING** THE MILKY CELLS WITH **LIGHT**

TO **CODIFY** THE **NIGHT** .

33-73

Survival

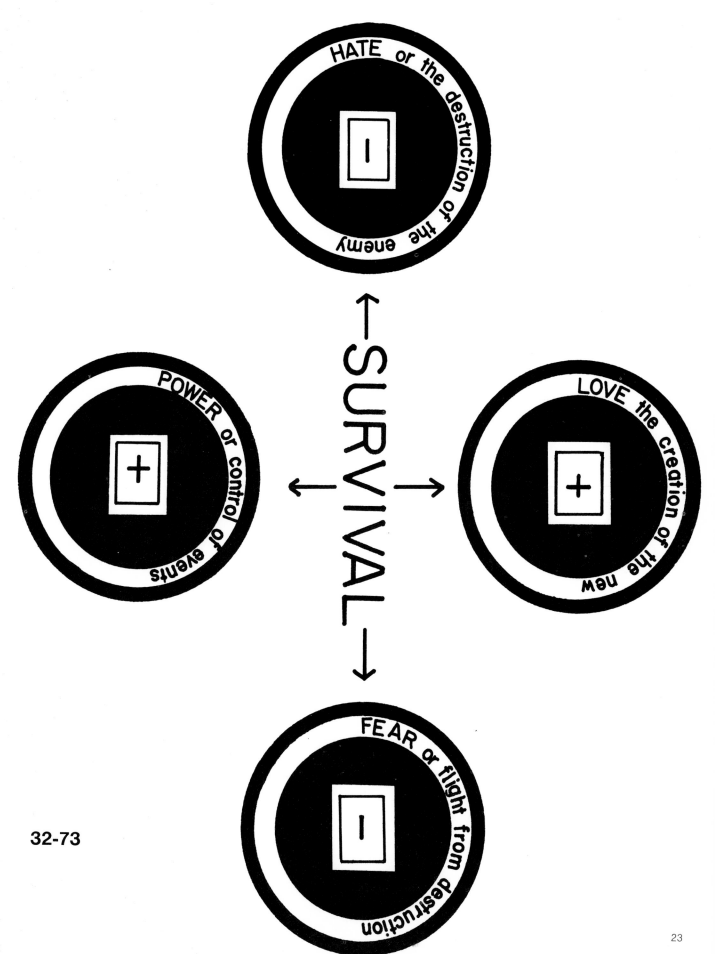

32-73

1933 The March of the Old Whores

TO THE CLICKING OF CONCRETE BY THE POPULATION'S HEELS

TO THE POUNDING ON THE PAVEMENTS OF THE TEEMING CITY STREETS

A DETERMINED RHYTHM BEATS:

EAT, EATS, EATS!

HOW MUCH FOR A WIFE?

HOW MUCH FOR A SON?

HOW MUCH FOR A WORK OF ART?

HOW MUCH TO MAKE THE LOVERS PART?

HOW MUCH FOR HONOR THAT YOU **THINK** THAT YOU HAVE WON?

GOING

GOING

GONE

OH HONEY, WITH YOUR LITTLE SUBWAY QUICKS

WON'T YOU WITH YOUR SWEETS, LITTLE SWEET MAN,

BUZZ THE MOLLS FOR MY —

EATS, EATS, EATS!

I SLEPT INSIDE THE SEWER IN THE SLUDGE,

HEARD THE GRAY LEGS ARGUE IN THE FLOP HOUSE WITH THE LICE,

PEDDLED ALL MY ASS HAD IN IT ON THE STREETS,

THEN BUNKED WHERE WHEEZY NAGS IN HAY BARNS

COUGHED ABOVE THE MICE.

THIS ISN'T JUST THE OUTCRY OF A GRUDGE.

IT'S CURIOSITY TO SEE

WHAT THE FUCK HAVE YOU TO GIVE — AND WHAT'S **YOUR** PRICE

FOR

EATS,

EATS,

EATS!

Continued . . .

1933 March of the Old Whores, continued . . .

WHEN I WAS YOUNG I WONDERED ONCE HOW LIFE COULD RUN
NOT JUST IN BUCKS, BUT IN OUR BLOOD
THROUGH BREAD, MILK, GREENS, COFFEE, AND MEAT,
BROUGHT DOWN TO US ON HIGHWAYS FROM THE SUN.
BUT SINCE I LEARNED YOU GET THE CLINK UNLESS THE JINGLE RINGS
I DON'T GIVE A SHIT FOR ANYTHING —
BUT EATS....

EATS,
EATS!

33

Defeat 1935

A LONGSHOREMAN WITH A PERFECT NOTE

WHOSE TONE CAN BREAK A CUP

EXPLAINED THE SOCIAL MAKE OF BUMS

"BUMS ARE WORKERS WHO GAVE UP"

35

After the Kill

G◁▷ZING IN THE **GLAZ**ED VISTAS

OF A DEAD RABBIT'S EYES

SUC**CESS**IONS OF RE**CESS**IONS OF HO**RIZ**ONS ═══ND

STILL . . . . THEY SEEM TO B═══

WITH THE PANIC PATTER AND THE ANGUISH OF THE SCATTERING FEET

IN A MUSCLE – FROZEN ST◁▷RE TOWARDS EMPTY SKIES . . . . .

GLASSY . . . . WITH TERROR GAMBLING ON RETREAT

THEN . . . . I ASK ┆S THE M^EA T

WORTH SUCH D^ESPERATE DEFE^A T

36-73

Iced Flits

WHERE THE NORTHERN LIGHTS

SEEMED TO CONDENSE

IN THE SMALL BALL

OF A SILVER FOX

FLICKERING THROUGH

DARK SPRUCE

I CAUGHT A MINK

IN A CRYSTAL CAVE

37-59-73

Once Upon a Trappers Cabin

Where

Tree—sticks hold up the dome

And winds pile up white barricades

There . . . .

Loneliness and snow can make a grave .

37-73

Two Gentle Arts

THE GENTLE ART OF **FUCKING**

AND FUR **TRAPPING**

DEPEND ON **LURES**

UNTIL . . . .

TRAPS SNAP THEIR **JAWS**

ON **FOXES** AND **MINK**

SPOUSES AND **WHORES**

39-73

Sleeping on My Hand

SLEEPING ON MY HAND

ITS MY FORGOTTEN THAT ABSOLVES MY SORROW,
SO PARDON ME FOR SLEEPING ON MY HAND;
OR IGNORING MORE THAN TWO AND FOUR TENTH MILES
OF TURDS
FLUSHING THRU MY LIFE POLLUTION IN THE LAND.
FOR WHEN I RESURRECT ORIGINATIONS OF MY WASTE
IN FORMS OF ANIMALS I TRAPPED AND ATE
I FEEL, WHEN DYING, I'LL SEE THEM WALK
ACROSS MY BED,
STARING AT ME IN UNSMILING FEAR.... STARK WITH HATE.
THEN, I WISH I'D **NOT** BEEN BORN....OR IF SO...DEAD.
AGAINST OUR GUILT AND GRIEF FOR LIFE'S DEFECTIONS
WHAT BUT FORGETFULNESS REPRIEVES REPENTENCE ?

41-73

REFLECTIONS ON PSYCHOLOGY, DESPAIR, AND FUR TRAPPING

There are several influences that predetermined the poems in this section.

A crucial influence came from the concepts of Dr. W. B. Cannon's physiological study of the emotions. Dr. Cannon related emotions to survival *on a physical not a metaphysical* basis. The great depression taught me the materialist positions of Marxism, the paranoias of Stalinism, and the political unreliability of liberals. Other influences were studies of symbolic logic, working as a sand riddler, ship scraper, and longshoreman, as well as the need to put meat on the table by catching furbearers.

These experiences crystalized my policy for existence. This was to *maximize* physical experiences; pattern formation and recognition; and, most important, the emotions of survival. These attitudes pervade all our compositions and contrast negative themes with positive expressions. The ways of writing can be a life style.

Note:

the three doctors in "Lines to Three Doctors" refer to

Dr. Walter Bradford Cannon, author of "Bodily Changes in Pain, Hunger, Fear, and Rage."

Dr. G. W. Crile, his co-worker in discovering adrenalin.

Dr. Linus Pauling.

Under Cheyenne Mountain

UNDER CHEYENNE MOUNTAIN A COLONEL SAID,

"THE FIRST DAY   OF NUCLEAR ATTACK

HALF OUR POPULATION WILL BE DEAD

THEN WE'LL REBUILD   WHAT 'S LEFT HERE."

SIR, "WHO COULD L——VE   WITH SUCH A LOSS?"

AGAIN THE COLONEL SAID,

69-73

If We Could Hear

IF I COULD **SPEAK** THE **LANGUAGE**

OF THE **LEMMINGS**

AND **ASK** A **LEMMING** HOW UNHAPPY

HE M^USt BE

TO **NEED** TO **WALK** I^nTO THE **SEA** . . . .

I **WON**DER ^IF WE'D H_EA^R:

72

Epilogue to a Divorce

DON'T MAKE ME OUT A **NAS**TY BASTARD

PITY MY CONTEMPT AND SNEER

CONSIDER   I TOOK A **LOT** OF SHIT FROM **YOU**

AND . . . . .

72

Dialogue with a Freight Agent in the Reading R.R. Station

CHECKED BAGGAGE , ICE CREAM MIXES,

AND REMAINS OF DECEASED PERSONS

REGARDLESS OF COMBINATION, SIZE

OR MEASURE ;

WHETHER DRESSED, NAKED OR TAGGED

FOR PLEASURE

WILL NOT BE HANDLED BY THE READING CO.

EITHER TO OR FROM PHILADELPHIA

Reading Company

"THIS POSTER SEEMS A LITTLE QUEER"

"THATS A GOOD QUESTION MAM

BUT...

I

ONLY WORK

HERE

70-73

Finale

WHY DO WE ONLY WORK HERE

THAT'S A GOOD QUESTION

65-72

COMMENTS ON
I ONLY WORK HERE

You know what we mean by
"I ONLY WORK HERE"

Snob Hill

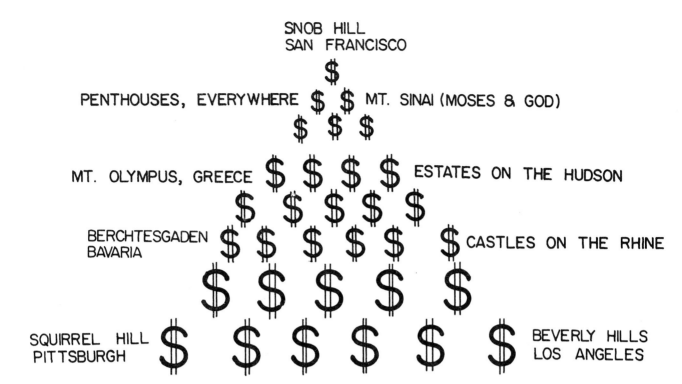

SNOB HILL
SAN FRANCISCO

$

PENTHOUSES, EVERYWHERE $ $ MT. SINAI (MOSES & GOD)

$ $ $

MT. OLYMPUS, GREECE $ $ $ $ ESTATES ON THE HUDSON

$ $ $ $ $

BERCHTESGADEN
BAVARIA $ $ $ $ $ $ CASTLES ON THE RHINE

$ $ $ $ $

SQUIRREL HILL
PITTSBURGH $ $ $ $ $ BEVERLY HILLS
LOS ANGELES

UNDER ef TINTO CLIMES WITH CIRRUS FRILLS

THE UPPER CLAW$S LIVES ON TOPS OF HILLS

TO LOOK DOWN
ON PEOPLE BELOW

TO SPY ON MORE THAN STANDARD DEVIATIONS FROM THE NORM

IN PRAYERS OF FLIES ON WINDOW PANES BEFORE THE STORM

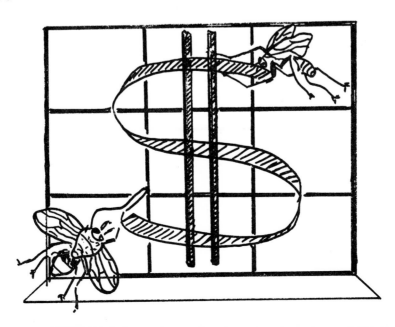

58-73

A Cloud Above the Hill

WHEN YOUNG AND UNEMPLOYED
I TOOK A RECESS FROM THE RACKET...
AND DISCUSSED THE UNIVERSE
WITH THE PITTSBURGH UNEMPLOYED.

BENEATH A RAILROAD TRESTLE
EAST OF SQUIRREL HILL
WE STOOD... AND TALKED
WHEN THE RATTLERS DIDN'T ROAR
OR WAITED MONTHS FOR WORK
AT JONES & LAUGHLIN'S MILL
SOME SAID, " WE NEED A WAR."

LATER.....I MET THEIR GHOSTS
ON TINIAN ISLAND WINGS
OVER FALLING WALLS OF NAGASAKI
THERE ... BY CAVED IN GIRDERS
OF THE MITSUBISHI STEEL WORKS
I SAW THEM DRINKING SAKI
OVER SIXTY THOUSAND CORPSES
SURELY,.....I THOUGHT,
THEIR GHOSTS WOULD FEEL REMORSE.

Continued...

A Cloud Above the Hill, continued . . .

SO I OFFERED THEM " WE **NEED** A **WAR**" WITH **WINE**

UNDER **REMNANTS** OF A **SHINTO** SHRINE . . .

DREAMING THEY WOULD **EAT** THEIR **WORDS**

INSTEAD . . . I SAW UNIVERSAL **POWER** RECYCLING

IN **HANDS** OF **APES** MERRILY **BICYCLING** .

THEY **SEEMED** SO **CLEVER** . . . . . TOO .

45-55-73

WAR DEPARTMENT STATEMENT
"The best interests of the United States require
the utmost co-operation by all concerned in
keeping secret *now and for all time in the
future* all scientific and technical information
not given in this report or other official
releases."

N.Y. TIMES, Aug. 12, 1945

Under a Cloud Below the Hill

SECURITY LIFE

THE MILITARY ENGINEERS
WITH NO WHISKERS IN THEIR EARS,
BUT NARROW EYES ABOVE THEIR SNEERS...
THEIR LIPS ARE THIN AS STITCHES.
UNDER THE HILLS THEY'RE SET TO BE INTERNED
UNTIL HALF OUR PEOPLE WILL HAVE BURNED
THEY'RE RATS: THOSE SONS OF WITCHES.

THE PURITAN ENGINEERS
FULL OF GAMMA RAY FEARS
WITH FACES SHORN....SEVERE
THEY WEAR GRAPHITE BREECHES
TO SHIELD THEIR BALLS BEHIND STONE WALLS
THE PSALM – SINGING SONS OF BITCHES.

THE POLITICAL SLIDE RULE JOCKS
WHO SLEEP IN SHALE – CUT DITCHES
THEY SLAP THEIR COCKS
ON ORDOVICIAN ROCKS,
TRYING TO LIVE FOREVER,
THE LOUSY SONS OF BITCHES.

59-73

Over the Hill in a Cloud

```
A
N
N              G        B        L   F      F
I              R    D   I        N   U      I
THE  POWER  OF  SUNS
L              W    A   T        T   O      O
A              T    T   H        E   N      N
T              H    H            H
I                               I
O                               N
N                               G
                                N
                                E
                                S
                                S
```

THE POWER OF SUNS

ANNIHILATION — GROWTH — DEATH — BIRTH — LITE — NITE — THINGNESS — FUSION — FISION

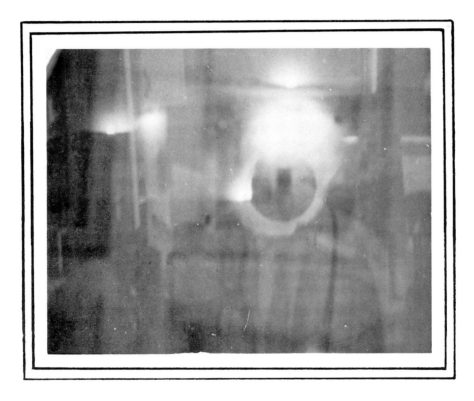

"THE DOVES OF PEACE RIDE ON THE ATOM"

STATEMENT BY 6ᵗʰ REGIMENT, 2ⁿᵈ MARINE DIVISION OFFICER
NAGASAKI SEPT. 1945

"IT(the atomic bomb) COULD MEAN THE END OF WAR AND AGGRESSION"

STALIN 8/08/'45   "STALIN" by MONTGOMERY HYDE   1972

45-73

**CONSIDERING
"HOT CLOUD HILL"**

EXPENDABLES

World War I — 11,000,000 dead
World War II — 20,000,000 dead

OH SAY CAN YOU FEEL

a light year?
a parsec?
a megaparsec?

17 Noises in the Testicles of an Old Giant

RORGZ   RORGZ

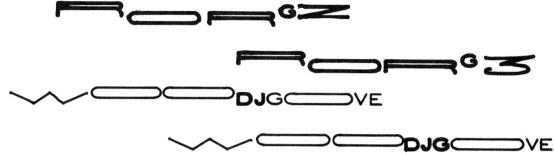

WOODJGOVE   WOODJGOVE   WOODJGOVE

ZADWEK   GADWAWK

MERLFRAKE   MERLFRAKE

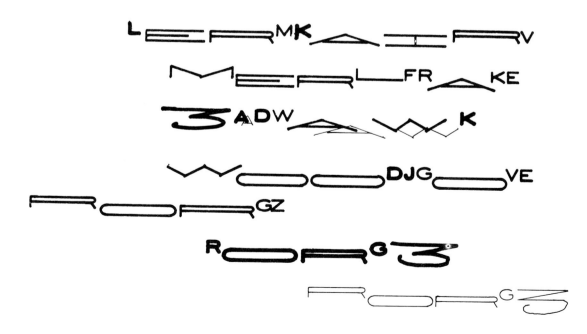

Out of Aeons

Silk of the Winds

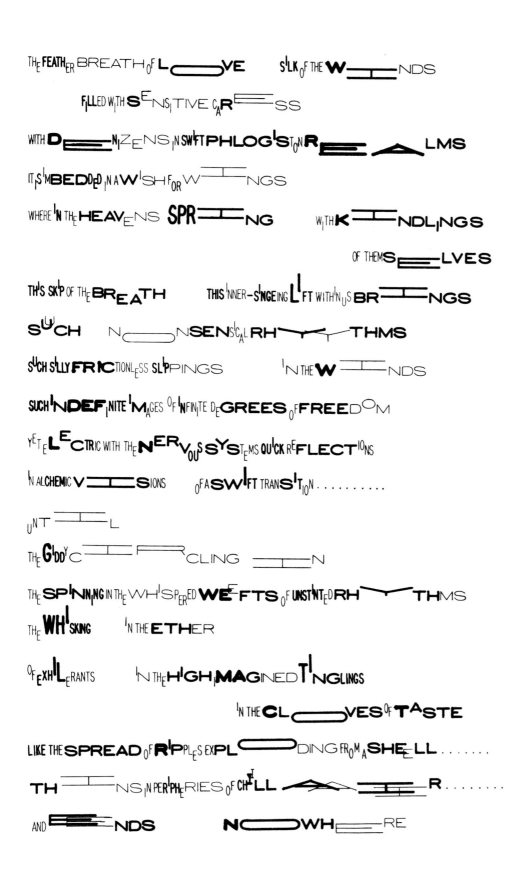

THE FEATHER BREATH OF LOVE   SILK OF THE WINDS

FILLED WITH SENSITIVE CARESS

WITH DENIZENS IN SWIFT PHLOGISTON REALMS

IT'S IMBEDDED IN A WISH FOR WINGS

WHERE IN THE HEAVENS SPRING   WITH KINDLINGS

OF THEMSELVES

THIS SKIP OF THE BREATH   THIS INNER-SINGEING LIFT WITHIN US BRINGS

SUCH   NONSENSICAL RHYTHMS

SUCH SILLY FRICTIONLESS SLIPPINGS   IN THE WINDS

SUCH INDEFINITE IMAGES OF INFINITE DEGREES OF FREEDOM

YET ELECTRIC WITH THE NERVOUS SYSTEMS QUICK REFLECTIONS

IN ALCHEMIC VISIONS   OF A SWIFT TRANSITION . . . .

UNTIL

THE GIDDY CIRCLING IN

THE SPINNING IN THE WHISPERED WEFTS OF UNSTINTED RHYTHMS

THE WHISKING   IN THE ETHER

OF EXHILERANTS   IN THE HIGH IMAGINED TINGLINGS

IN THE CLOVES OF TASTE

LIKE THE SPREAD OF RIPPLES EXPLODING FROM A SHELL . . . .

THINS IN PERIPHERIES OF CHILL AIR . . . .

AND ENDS   NOWHERE

40-72

Pledge

I SAID TO LIVE IN PRIVACY

NEVER LET ME TRY

TO IMITATE WITH GLASS

YOUR BRIGHT IMAGINED EYES

SO MAY OUR TRIP GO

TO OUR MADNESS TOO

WITH STRANGE MUSIC TO ACCOMPANY

THE SERENDIPITY

OF OUR CREATIVITY

AND SO SUSTAIN

OUR PRIVACY

42-70

Whisper Composition

RUMBLES

OF SUN STORMS

CASCADE

THROUGH   WHITE NOONS

WHEN RESURRECTIONS   ONESTER-BREATHS

IN SPRING RAIN   EVOKE THIS REFRAIN

WHO   ON TIPTOES   WHISPERS   TO ME

OUT OF THE NIGHTS   THE DELICACY OF DISTANCE

PUTS MORNING STILLNESS ON THE MOTH

QUIET AS LIGHT   ON OUR LIPS

66-72

ECHOES FROM 17 NOISES
IN THE TESTICLES
OF AN OLD GIANT

There are more ways than you can dream of for a man and woman to relate besides the five ways in this section.

Will privacy be forgotten like the sex hospitality in the Eskimo igloos? Forgotten like the aphrodisiacs and love philters of the Congo and India, or the love charm in the wings of the black butterfly in the drum of the Zuni dancers, awakening desire with phallic gourds?

Who's that hooded woman under the rock of Cogul?

SECTION 5
Cosmic Blips and Whens

$$\boxed{(\overline{A}):(B)} : \{A:(A+\overline{B})\} :: \boxed{(B+A):\overline{B}}$$

SEPTEMBER CAME FLOATING

WITH   ITS STARS AMOONG THE WALNUTS

WHEN THE SHADOW OF THE ROCK FALLS
TOOWARDS AUTUMN . . . . . .
                    IN THE TREE

STARS   ARE   BESIIDES   THE WALNUTS

WHEN SEPTEMBER'S SHADOW SHOOWS THEM

OON   THE TREE

62-73

Again of the When

IN THEIR TOWERS

THE CLOCKS KEEP RUNNING

INSPITE OF THE WINDS

25-71

More Than Two Agains of the When

IS IT THE FEVER

OR FINGERLING WHISPERS

OR JUST MOON-TICKS

THAT KEEP SALMON RUNNING

INSPITE OF THE R————FFS

IS IT INVENTION

OR RIGOR OF METALS

OR CELESTIAL INTENTION

THAT KEEP CLOCKS RUNNING

INSPITE OF THE W————NDS

25-72

The Veil

WHEN I AL────NE INSIDE OF DARKNESS ON A H════LL

FEEEL THE S════LENCE OF THE VE════════L

HOW SPACE EQU────TES IMMENSITY WITH SILENCE

AND TIME P────LES THE VEIIL

THEN I WISH I **COULD** BELIEEVE.....OR EVEN GUESS

THE UNIVERSE "REM════MBERS"

AS THO IT SPUN AN EPITAPH OF GAS

WITH REMNANTS ────F...... AND T────AS L────N

OR..... ABS────F────RBING ═══N

THE MORE EN────F────RMOUS QUIETNESS OF GALACTIC DISTANCES

THOUGHTS IN A MAN ALONE IN THE NIGHT

PONDERING.......────N.......A S════LENCE────N.......

A WREATH OF LIGHT

61-73

A Rare Escape May Be Beautiful

WHEN RUBY ANTARES

GRAZING   THE MOON

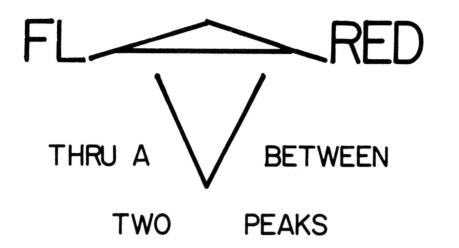

FL⟁RED

THRU A   BETWEEN

TWO   PEAKS

" THE GIANTS CAUGHT LIGHTNING IN A BOTTLE "

AND FR═══D IT . . . . . . INAFLASH

70-72

Abstraction

considering:

the irretrievability of a photon,

velocity = $2.99793 \times \dfrac{10,000,000,000 \text{ cm.}}{1 \text{ sec.}}$

OR

the invisibility of individual electrons

mass = $9.1085 \times \dfrac{1 \text{ gm.}}{10,000,000,000,000,000,000,000,000,000}$

angels seldom perspire

and never use toilet paper

69-72

Death of the Sun

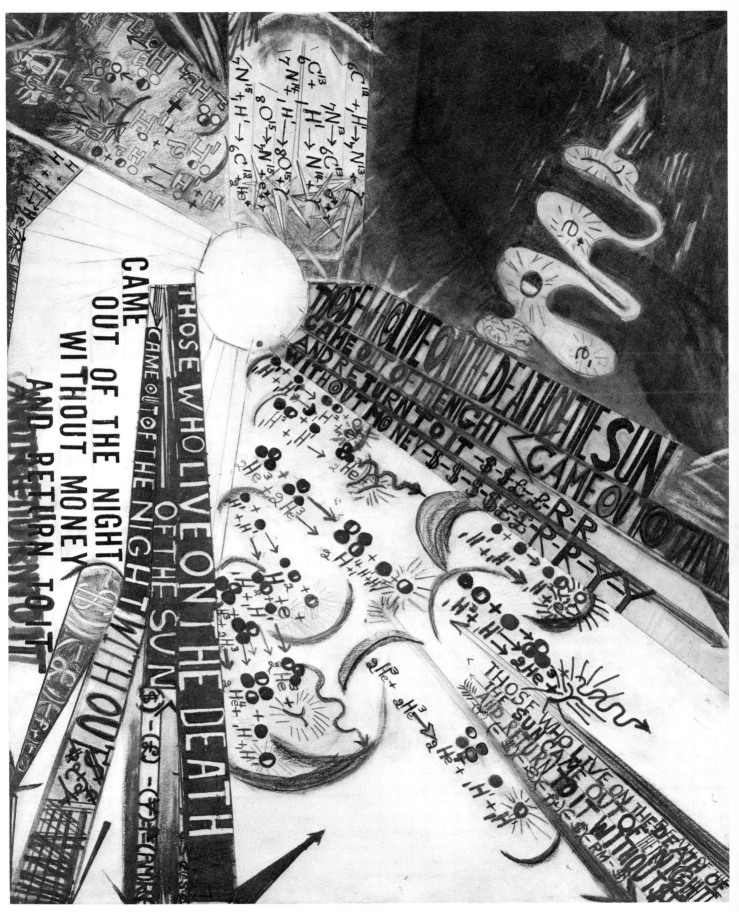

71

Geiger Counter Speaks Of

Geiger Counter Speaks Of

THE CURSE

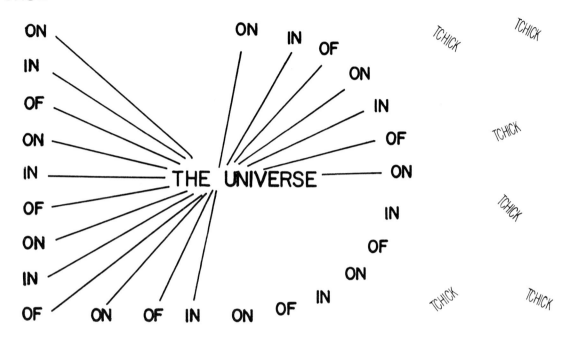

TCHICK TCHICK TCHICK TCHICK TCHICK TCHICK TCHICK TCHICK TCHICK

TCHICK TCHICK TCHICK TCHICK TCHICK   TCHICK TCHICK TCHICK.   TCHICK

56-73

The Source of Imperfection

WHILE THE NIGHT SKY SHINES WITH MASS DESTRUCTION

SO CREATION CAN SELF-GENERATE

THE DYING SUNS RAISE A DEEP QUESTION:

IS THE UNIVERSE A HUGE MISTAKE?

IF NOT WHY CANT EXISTENCE BE FREED

FROM ITS NEED TO SELF-ANNIHILATE?

72

FORESHADOWED BY COSMIC BLIPS AND WHENS

How would you like living in an all-electric cosmic energy culture, beautiful as sunlight, clean as filtered and distilled geothermal steam, steady as a star? A boring steady-state existence broken by the sporadicism of windmills. Or would you prefer howling at the moon in the Fiesta of the Cannibals?

Happiness with emptiness . . .   to end emptiness

JESUS CHRIST

Blessed ARE the POOR in spirit: for theirs is the
Kingdom of Heaven

The Beatitudes, St. Matthew 5, No 3

MAO TSE-TUNG

To the 7th Central Committee of the Communist Party
of China, 3/05/'49
"In Reality its a good thing that China's 600 million people
are "poor and blank". Poverty gives rise to the desire for
Action; the desire for Change; and the desire for Revolution."

PLATO

The Mother of the God "LOVE" was Penia or Poverty who
conceived "LOVE" with the GOD POROS or Plenty in the
Garden of Zeus at the feast for Aphrodite. Poverty came
to the party to beg and found Poros lying in the grass,
sleeping off too many drinks of nectar. There she seduced
Plenty to end her Penury.

The Symposium, B. Jowett translation, p. 332,
Vol. III.

24-72

Happiness with emptiness . . .   for emptiness

INDEPENDENT OF DESIRES, PASSIONS AND CYCLES OF EXISTENCE. NIRVANA: A SUBJECTIVE STATE THAT APPROACHES ABSOLUTE NOTHINGNESS

ONE ATOM PER CUBIC METER IS THE DENSITY OF INTERGALACTIC SPACE

MERGING WITH AN INFINITY OF EMPTINESS AT ONE WITH THE UNIVERSE. NIRVANA: A STATE OF MIND

AVERAGE DISTANCE BETWEEN TWO STARS IS LIKE FORTY MILES BETWEEN TWO RAINDROPS

73

Unhappiness with emptiness . . .

IT IS A VANISHING SELF – CENTER

WITHOUT BOUNDARIES;

A STATE

THAT SHOWS NO COMPONENT OF WHITE,

NOR IS IT WHITE.

IT HAS NO SOUND

NO ODOR.

NOR CAN A BLIND MAN

FEELING HIS WAY ACROSS AN EMPTY LAWN

STUMBLE AGAINST IT

IN THE NIGHT.

26-72

Happiness with emptiness... 	in blankness and white

After discussing the revolutionary
potential in the poverty of the
Chinese people who are "poor and blank"
Mao Tse—Tung associated poetry
with political leadership:
"On a blank sheet of paper
free from any mark,
the freshest and most beautiful
characters can be written,
the freshest and most beautiful
pictures can be painted."

Report to the 7th Central Committee
of the Communist Party of China
(3 / 1 / 49)
Selected Works Vol. IV p.369

Happiness with emptiness... in black

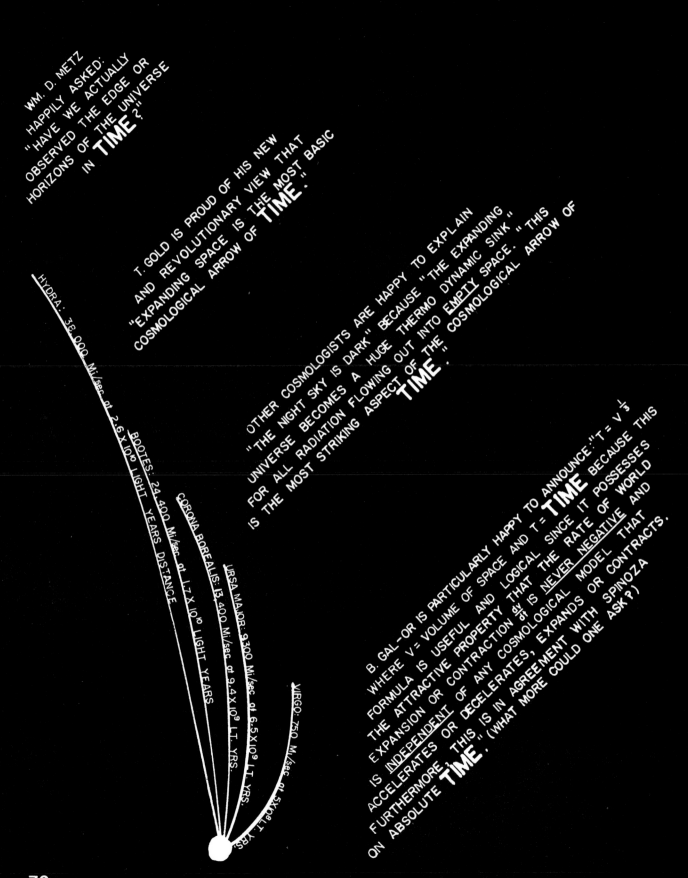

WM. D. METZ HAPPILY ASKED: "HAVE WE ACTUALLY OBSERVED THE EDGE OR HORIZONS OF THE UNIVERSE IN **TIME**?"

T. GOLD IS PROUD OF HIS NEW AND REVOLUTIONARY VIEW THAT "EXPANDING SPACE IS THE MOST BASIC COSMOLOGICAL ARROW OF **TIME**."

OTHER COSMOLOGISTS ARE HAPPY TO EXPLAIN "THE NIGHT SKY IS DARK" BECAUSE "THE EXPANDING UNIVERSE BECOMES A HUGE THERMO DYNAMIC SINK" FOR ALL RADIATION FLOWING OUT INTO <u>EMPTY</u> SPACE." THIS IS THE MOST STRIKING ASPECT OF THE COSMOLOGICAL ARROW OF **TIME**."

HYDRA: 38,000 Mi/sec at 2.6 X 10⁹ LIGHT YEARS DISTANCE

BOOTES: 24,400 Mi/sec at 1.7 X 10⁶ LIGHT YEARS DISTANCE

CORONA BOREALIS: 13,400 Mi/sec at 1.7 X 10¹⁰ LIGHT YEARS

URSA MAJOR: 9300 Mi/sec at 9.4 X 10⁹ LT. YRS.

VIRGO: 750 Mi/sec at 6.5 X 10⁹ LT. YRS.

....at 1.5 X 10⁸ LT. YRS.

B. GAL–OR IS PARTICULARLY HAPPY TO ANNOUNCE:"T = V^⅓ WHERE V= VOLUME OF SPACE AND T = **TIME** BECAUSE THIS FORMULA IS USEFUL AND LOGICAL SINCE IT POSSESSES THE ATTRACTIVE PROPERTY THAT THE RATE OF WORLD EXPANSION OR CONTRACTION $\frac{dv}{dt}$ IS <u>NEVER NEGATIVE</u> AND IS <u>INDEPENDENT</u> OF ANY COSMOLOGICAL MODEL THAT ACCELERATES OR DECELERATES, EXPANDS OR CONTRACTS. FURTHERMORE, THIS IS IN AGREEMENT WITH SPINOZA ON ABSOLUTE **TIME**." (WHAT MORE COULD ONE ASK?)

Happiness with emptiness . . .   in black and white

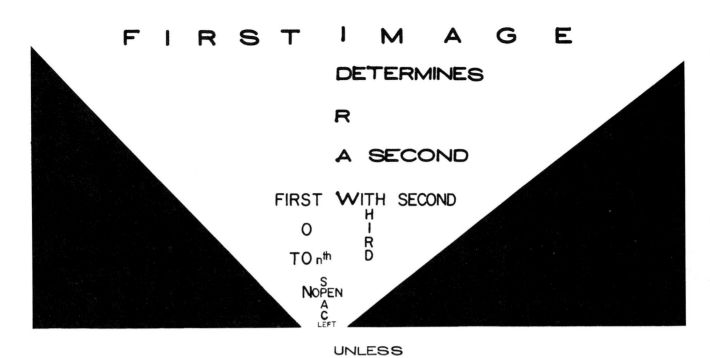

FIRST IMAGE

DETERMINES

R

A SECOND

FIRST WITH SECOND

O

TO nth

NO OPEN SPACE LEFT

UNLESS

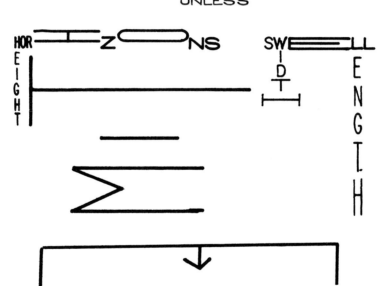

WHEN WHITE SPACE

SPREADS

CREATION

Happiness with emptiness ...   as anti-density

THE NIGHT-SKY IS SO LOVELY

WHAT A PITY WE MUST DIE

COULD WE EVER GET ITS MESSAGE

UNLESS IT WERE SO EMPTY

71-73

HOW COME HAPPINESS
WITH EMPTINESS?

Once during a young man I decided that if our culture had any universal character at all it was in our scientific industrial domain. All else seemed froth. What should a poet do?

Follow Boris Slutsky, the Soviet poet?

"Physicists are somehow much in honor
Lyricists are somehow pushed aside.
It's not a question of cold calculation:
It's just a question of universal law."
"That's why physicists are held in honor,
That's why lyricists are pushed aside."

That's why I became a chemist to be a poet; a poet to be an astronomer; an astronomer to write universally as a poet...a poet to put back into the *desubjectivized Universals of physics or astrophysics* some of the subjestivity taken out.

For this I've been called a madman. So I contemplate HAPPINESS WITH EMPTINESS in vacua 50,000 times more exhaustive than our laboratories can produce. And when the calendar is imprecise by hours I return to the FEAST OF FOOLS.

Ecology

IT IS MY IGNORANCE I DO ENJOY
SO PARDON ME FOR PISSING ON WHITE SAND

73

Ecce: Saprosondgy

THE **FAMILY** WAS **WIPED** OUT
BY AN **ATTACK** OF **SAPROSONDGY**....
A **CRY** IN A **DARK** CLOUD.

SHE WAS INSTRUCTED BY **SAPROSONDGY** :
" **OPEN** YOUR **MOUTH** AND **STARE** ."

LATER ....ON **SATURDAY** AFTERNOONS
THE **CHEERING** SECTION **CHANTED** :
SAPROSONDGY   SAPROSONDGY

THEN .... DOCTOR **GRANT** PUBLISHED :
"A **CORRELATION** BETWEEN **SAPROSONDGY**
                AND **TYOXDAX** "
THAT SHOWED AN **UNCERTAINTY** < 0.0001
WITH A **POWERFUL** ARGUMENT FOR FURTHER **RESEARCH**
SUPPORT OF ONE MILLION DOLLARS
TO DETERMINE THEIR **SYNERGY**
IN THE CURE FOR **COMPULSIVE** EATING.

FINALLY :
THIS .... BROUGHT DOWN **RAIN** FROM DARK CLOUDS ;
COMPASSION FOR THE **SAPROSONDGY** VICTIMS ;
TAUGHT HER TO SHUT HER **MOUTH** ;
GAVE **VICTORY** TO THE **HOME** TEAMS ;
OBTAINED HIS **MILLION DOLLAR FUND**

Continued ...

Ecce: Saprososodngy, continued . . .

FOR DOCTOR **GRANT**;

AND MADE THE FAT GREEK **RESTAURANT** OWNERS,
MISTER AND MRS. **TYOXDAX**

THE **HAPPIEST** PARENTS IN THE **DEVELOPMENT**

AMEN

62-72

Questions for Stochastic Artists

AREN'T YOU THE P[===]MPS OF THE STOCK MARKET

R[/\===]NBOWS OF **BOARD**ROOM **J**E**R**KS

NONSENSE THE **RICH** MAN **BART**ER**ED**

FOR **DOL**LARS L[===]SING THEIR WORTH

HOW ARE YOUR SEN**S**[/\]TIONS AS **SPEC**UL[/\]TIONS

DO YOUR EM[===]TIONS

WAARRANT PROM[===]TIONS

WHEN YOU FL**OA**TED LONG H[/\===]RS

ON A L[===]NE DOWNST[/\===]RS

DID THE D**EA**D R'SE FROM THEIR GRA**V**ES

WAS G**E**N**I**US ON'T WHEN YOU **DROP**PED APE **VO**MIT

TO **PIC**TURE RANDOM W[/\]VES

DID YO**U** CONFL[___]SE YOUR **NOIS**ES . . . .WITH **CHOIC**ES

YOUR **LIFE** TH[===]ME . . . . .HOW M**U**CH IS IT W[===]RTH

U**N**DER SNOW OF **DICE** ON THE STOCK M**AR**K**ET**

'N RA**I**NBOWS OF **BOARD**ROOM **J**E**R**KS

67-73

Since Art Thrives

SINCE ART THRIVES
ON WHAT SOCIETY

FORBIDS OVERLOOKS AMBIGUATES OMITS

OR
blindly seeks

WHAT IS
more heady to expose
than symbols of the **IGNORANCE**
authorities impose
when poets and artists piss
publicly upon subverted rules
AT THE FEAST
OF FOOLS

73

The Feast of Fools

pretending with
instructing in
consoling for
regaling are

ALL WHAT THEY'RE NOT

the feast of fools

Openess

WHENEVER I HAVE **LEARNED** A **FACTY FACT**

I **WONDER**

WHAT **POSSIBILITIES**

MAY BE **ELIMINATED**

BY THAT **SENTIENT ACT** . . . .

AND . . . HOW MUCH **VALUE** FOR THE ONES

WHOM **IGNORANCE** LEAVES

DETACHED

73

Ephemeris

WITH MY HAND UPON MY SWEETHEART'S ASS

I WATCH THE SEASONS PASS

AMONG TEN PLANETS SWINGING

IN THE DUST-NET OF THE SUN.

BUT. . .SHOULD I SAY ALAS,

IT IS MY IGNORANCE TO ENJOY. . .YET IGNORE

MORE CHOICES IN THAT RING-DANCE OF THE SUN

THAN THE MATRIX OF MY BRAIN CAN STORE:

SO GRANT COMPASSION WHEN I DO CONFESS

IT IS MY IGNORANCE I DO ENJOY

AND PA H RDON ME FOR PISSING ON WHITE SAND

58-73

When Darkness Moves

THE HERMIT CRAB CARRIES A DARKNESS

ACROSS THE RADIANCE OF ITS BEACH,

A DARKNESS OF WEAKNESS MORE COHERENT

THAN THE LIGHT ON ITS CORAL REEF.

73

CONSIDER

When Darkness Moves

APPENDIX

SIDELIGHTS ON WORDS AND PHRASES

"The giants caught lightning in a bottle" p. 95, a remark by Jackie Robinson of the Brooklyn Dodger's baseball team when the New York Giants beat the Dodgers for the 1951 National League Pennant.

"The Feast of Fools", p. 137. The Feast of the Fools developed from Roman Saturnalia and Greek Dionysic festivals which also turned the social pyramid upside down and relaxed the people with one wild day of intoxication and free sex. This orgy of fun was enjoyed in Europe from the twelfth century to 1435 A.D. on Christmas or New Year's Day. It was sometimes called the "Feast of Asses" when the flight from Egypt was symbolized by walking a live ass into the church to the accompaniment of brayings and buffoonery. The Feast of Fools was presided over by a Lord of Misrule and a Bishop or Pope of Fools.

"Stochastic", p. 133 means any process of generating messages that depends on random operations such as flipping a coin or drawing numbers from a bowl. When John Cage selected successive musical notes from a random number book or Jackson Pollock, the painter, made "pictures" by splattering unpredictable color patterns across a canvas they were acting as "Stochastic Artists".

I wonder whether Cage and Pollock were so intent on unscrambling the restraints imposed by habits and rules of art in order to turn up unpredictable images and unusual music that they forgot or disregarded this fact of life. When physical symbols or signals are shuffled into complete disorder, human beings see nothing and hear only gibberish. If Cage and Pollock, *knowingly, purposely* disregarded our need to structure existence in order to relate to it, then they might have been paraphrasing the famous reply of the philosopher, Morris Cohen, to a student accusing him of destroying all her values, beliefs and her faith in life: "After I clean out the Augean Stables, why should I fill them up again?"

If We Could Hear, p. 47. Although Lemming populations disappear, they do not march into the sea. We retained the legendary image because its insight is true and myth-like. (Scientific American, 6/74, p. 38)

THE FOUR WAYS

We shall briefly summarize the four ways of writing English that appear throughout "I Only Work Here". The four ways are: Accents of Information, Table 1, p. 151; Prosodynic Orthography, Tables 2 & 3, pp. 152, 153; Visual and Concrete poetry which fragments English script and moves freely in all directions; and plain English text.

The problem in relating four kinds of styles to five decades of themes confronted me. They challenged the authors to consider the questions of graphic design, speech-music, linguistics, communication theory and semantics.

One general and possibly important conclusion can be stated. Due to 90% to 95% redundancy in oral English (about 80% in some texts) many themes can be expressed quite adequately in two of the four kinds of script. Yet no theme was equally well fitted to all four styles and some themes required one and only one style for appropriate expression. For instance: more abstract themes that lacked emotion were more perfectly written with strictly visual script in the style of concrete poetry. Themes with complex feelings, varying intensity of emotion, subtle and suggestive patterns of taste and highly variable tempos found their best fit with prosodynic script. These were the themes that demanded *extra work* on the part of the reader, i.e. extra attention. When we intended the reader to do *less work*, then script displaying accents of information was written. Accents of information increase the size of a word according to the amount of information it carries.

Accents of information, a sort of poetry-speed-read style, were most effective for a longer composition or for those abstract themes clarified by featuring, graphically, the author's intent.

TABLE 1
Accents of Information

Grammatic Unit	Order of Stress.	Frequency of Occurrence of Different Words.	Measure of Information
NOUNS	4	1,029 dif. noun words / 11,660 all noun words	0.0885
VERBS	3	456 dif. verb words / 12,550 all verb words	0.0364
ADJECTIVES* ADVERBS* AUXILIARY VERBS PRONOUNS CONJUNCTIONS PREPOSITIONS	2	188 ave. dif. words / 12,407 ave. all words	0.0143
ARTICLES AND REDUCED VOWELS	1	3 dif. article words / 5,550 all article words	0.0005

MECHANICAL Accents of Information

WHILE THE **NIGHT SKY** SHINES WITH MASS **DESTRUCTION**

SO **CREATION** CAN SELF – GENERATE

THE DYING **SUNS** RAISE A DEEP **QUESTION** :

IS THE **UNIVERSE** A HUGE **MISTAKE** ?

IF NOT WHY CANT **EXISTENCE** BE FREED

FROM ITS **NEED** TO SELF – ANNIHILATE ?

INTENTIONAL Accents of Information

WHILE THE NIGHT SKY **SHINES** WITH **MASS DESTRUCTION**

SO **CREATION CAN** SELF – GENERATE

THE **DYING** SUNS RAISE A DEEP **QUESTION** :

IS THE **UNIVERSE** A HUGE **MISTAKE** ?

IF **NOT** WHY CANT EXISTENCE BE **FREED**

FROM ITS NEED TO **SELF - ANNIHILATE** ?

* From: French, Carter & Koenig, "Words and Sounds in Telephone Conversations" Bell Telephone Monograph, B-491, 6/1930.

4 NOTES ON TABLE 1

1. Readers of Table 1 will notice asterisks next to "adjectives" and "adverbs". Observations showed that the dependency of adjectives on nouns, and adverbs on the verb they modify, reduces the amount of information calculated by frequency of occurrence. Therefore the rank of adjectival and adverbial information has been lowered below the information level of verbs. This is not surprising, since the amount of information of symbols is a function of their independence as well as their frequency of occurrence.

2. The reader should realize the limited applicability of statistics to single occurrences. That is why the freely selected intentional accents of information, when *decisions of the poet* determine the size of a word, give an extra dimension to the mechanical formula on Table I. This does not invalidate the linguistic significance of mechanical accents of information, nor their use as guides.

3. This Bell Telephone study of 80,000 recorded words reported only 3% were different words. The 97% redundancy figure is in line with Leigh Lisker's 94% redundancy for monosyllabic words reported by the Haskin's Laboratory, S-R-10(1967).

4. The data on articles in the Bell Laboratory report has been compared with the frequency of occurrence of articles in a 1955 study of spontaneous speech by air force students at Ohio State University by J. W. Black and M. Ausherman. The difference was 1.9%. See "The Vocabulary of College Students", Bureau of Educational Research, Ohio State University, 1955.

TABLE 2
Prosodynes - Code Goth III

DURATION

Trace

A E I O U   THE of

Short

AEOIUWY

Normal

A E I OU W Y

Prolonged

AEIOUY

INTENSITY

Whisper Level

a e i o u w y

Quiet Unaccented Speech
(First Amplitude Level)

A E I O U W Y

Normal Conversational Effort
(Second Amplitude Level)

A E I O U W Y

Maximum Stress or Intensity
(Third Amplitude Level)

A E I O U W Y

PITCH

Lowest Pitch —
indicated by depressing the Vowels.

MIM MOM MAWM MEEM

Middle Pitch —
indicated by normal position on line.

MIM MOM MAWM MEEM

Highest Pitch —
indicated by elevating the Vowels.

MIM MOM MAWM MEEM

PAUSES

Intra-phrase pause, articulatory:
blank space 2 times height of tallest letter.
Inter-phrase, for breath and syntax:
blank space 4 times height of tallest letter.
Pause of thought:
line of dots varying from 1 cm. to 3 cm. with
time for decision.
Pause allocations require some semantic
judgment by the writer.

TABLE 3
Cues for Vowel Pitch Modulation

Same Vowel Spoken with Rising or Falling
Pitch in Periods Controllable by Speaker

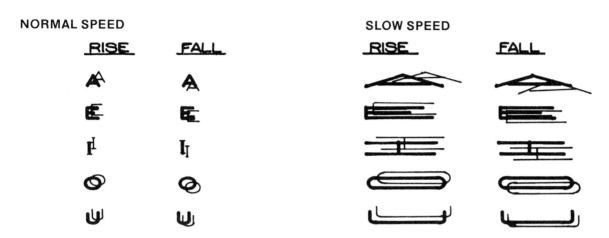

1 SAY...... DID YOU SEE **THAT** N⬭......YOU DIDN'T SEEE HER DO THE LOOP DE LOOP SHE'S A FIRE BALL WHAT A SHOW DO YOU WANT A BALLOON YEEHH

2 ITS INCREEE DIBLE I NEVER THOUGHT HED EVEN MAKE IT TO **FIRST** BASE YET THEERE HE S, LEADING THE PACK........... WHAT CAME OVER HIM WAS IT HORSE SHOES THEY SAY ITS BETTER TO BE LUCKY THAN GOOD

3 THERE'S NO RETUURN.......THAT CAN'T BEE HE WENT LIKE THAT IT WAS JUST YESTERDAY I SAW HIM

153

[(A):(B):{A:(A+B)}] :: [(B+A):B]
Notes on Ratios as Poetic Form.

A — Phrases or lines with references to time or of states of change. These expressions include no long-duration prosodynes.

B — Phrases or lines that identify situations where things are fixed in place with spatial relationship.

All "B" statements include two maximum duration prosodynes. The selection of these prosodynes was spontaneous. They just happened; they were not contrived.

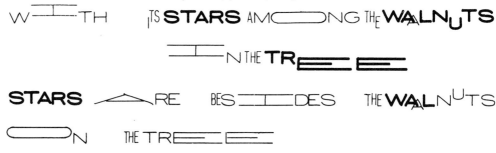

The [(A) : (B) : {A :(A+B)}] :: [(B+A) : B] form of proportions was clearly in mind before the poem was written and became the pattern or form of the composition.

The design of the poem opens the question of applicability of mathematical relations to poetry. It is the author's judgment that the following criteria must be satisfied if a mathematical form is to achieve poetic excellence.

(1) The images must be felt or observed. They must have personal subjective value.

(2) The theme must be sufficiently alive to the poet, emotionally, for the composition to have an empathy potential. The writing must be emotionally genuine and not just a mathematical trick.

(3) The components of the theme should be sufficiently general in meaning to "fit" the generality of mathematicl symbols...here space and time dimensions made the elementary mathematical treatment possible.

(4) The constraints of mathematical form should be justified by a contribution to the form of the poem such as elegance or simplicity of pattern.

TOWARDS INCREASING THE INFORMATION OF POETRY

The position taken here is: unless poetry is presented as a crossover, feedback art between its audio-vocal and visual-graphic domains its channels for information will not open up...its power for expression and its potentials for appeal will not be realized.

The visual information of poetry can be augmented by four kinds of script. Three of these appear in this book. They are modified template orthography; variations in size of print to convey four stress levels of information; and the fragmented, any-direction lines of so-called "concrete" poetry. A fourth script is the yet-to-be researched chirographic writing of the philosopher, Charles Saunders Peirce. Peirce called this script, "art chirography". He seems to suggest a transposition of hand-writing features associated with personality traits into a new psycho-graphic dimension for poetry.

Although some of these four shapes of script are taught in a scatter of locations, there is no single place where all four are offered to students. Possibly, an art school or art department would offer the most congenial atmosphere.

The greatest obstacle to presenting the audio-vocal information of poetry is the refusal of most academicians to rid themselves of a blindness that assumes prosody *must be confined* to two and only two kinds of stressed syllables: the weak and the strong. This position is rationalized on these grounds: some experiments show that listeners to spoken English are presented with acoustic signals carrying only two levels of stress, the stressed and the unstressed. P. Lieberman (WORD, No. 1, pp. 40-54)

Let us review the record. Over the years four levels of stress have been heard and marked by Joshua Steele, 1781; John Walker, 1808; Jesperson, 1907; Bloch and Trager, 1942; Trager and Smith, 1951; Gleason, 1961; Robson, 1963. I observed a 75% agreement on assignments of stress on syllables in the sentence, "A large sum of money was counted." Indirect confirmations came from measurements of speech power levels in telephone conversations, Fletcher, 1958; assessment of scanning levels on the basis of intrinsic speech power, Robson, 1959.

The need for 4 levels of stress in computer models of English prosody was verified in 1974 by Lt. D. C. Sargent, Purdue University, Indiana. J. Gaitensby, who specialized in prosodic research at Haskins laboratory for 14 years, stated that English prosody requires 4 levels of stress for a high fidelity rendition.

Continued ...

Why then should stress perceptions be enumerated sometimes as two, sometimes as four levels? The answer involves which stress component, what conditions for presenting the cues for stress, and what model of natural language is assumed. A most important consideration is what special uses of language are the interests of the experiment. If we look at natural language as a 95% redundant, multi-set of long and short, weak and strong cues, why should a listener pay attention to more than two levels of stress? Other cues will take care of comprehension in a 95% redundant conversation. But is poetry conversation? The reduced context in the parsimonious language of poetry increases the uncertainty of its symbols (Shannon 1951). Poetry creates new contexts of feeling; its own orders of redundancy.

Poetry is an art with a setting of its own; a pattern of words, phonemes, syllables and lines on a page; sometimes a shaping of the whole page, too. It has a text visibility that instructs reader-speakers to listen to its singular rhythms of speech. This is not the goal of naturalness that frequently prescribes texts for speech perception experiments. It is the reason for E. A. Robinson's lines:

"They are not ordinary frogs at all.
They are the frogs of Aristophanes."

For poets interested in information carried by prosody the limitations of a two level system is as nonsensical as though a singer were told, "Fundamental pitch of vowels in Englsih conversation carry little intelligibility and are minor influences on communication." (G. Miller 1951) Why then do you care to sing?

Accordingly, these proposals are advanced for the enrichment of poetry:

1. that stress first be writable as several "accents of information" measurable for unpredictability and operating as *graphic expressions* of intent, emphasis, and effort by the writer.

2. that the acoustic dimensions of stress, of its loudness levels relative to the average loudness of the talker, be writable with cues that instruct readers to speak relative levels of pitch and intensity with duration and pauses. These graphic cues on the page from the poet to the reader are called prosodynes, i.e. prosodic levels.

3. that vowel pitch modulations within a single syllable (rise-fall), (fall-rise), (steady-level) of tone languages become writable in English without rigid attachments of meaning to pitch levels as in tone languages.

Other perceptual and thematic roads to new information in poetry have been mentioned in the introduction p. 1 1 . The implications of all these suggestions may not be trivial. Were poetry to enter areas of enlarged perceptions it could relate individual self-expression to the information techniques of this culture. And its creative interests in the audio-vocal interactions with visual-graphic elements in writing can only deepen and broaden our understanding of natural languages. Originally the poet as "poeta", "poetei" was the maker, the inventor of language. Today we know that the modes of production in the hands of the people transmit and modify language. But this does not eliminate the poet as a valuable refiner of natural language as a whisper in history of its anonymous tides; a voice for survival; as a maker of verbal patterns that maximize suggestibility; and sometimes, in a quiet way, a composer who turns gabble into speech music for the enjoyment of song.

ACKNOWLEDGMENT

Dr. Leigh Lisker, chairman of the Linguistic Department, Univ. of Pennsylvania, generously made available his paper on the redundancy of oral monosyllabic words in English: (SR-10, 1967) Status Report on Speech Research, Haskins Laboratories, an irregular publication.

Photo Credits

Section 1   Author's Collection
Section 3   Official U.S. Marine Corps Photo
Section 6   Author's Collection
All others   Source unknown, believed to be
            U.P.I. or Wirephoto photographs.

Book design and layout, James Lowell Adams.